WHISPERS
FROM
JESUS

WHISPERS AND PRAYERS
FROM ABOVE

CASSANDRA LAWS

WHISPERS FROM JESUS

This book belongs to:

WHISPERS FROM JESUS

Dedicated to Jesus.

For his children. Thank you lord for your grace and mercy upon us.

Glory be to God.

Colossians 3:23

WHISPERS FROM JESUS

*Hold out your hand,
for Jesus Christ
holds the plan.*

Philippians 1:6

WHISPERS FROM JESUS
Introduction:

I gladly invite you to come and sit while you enjoy Jesus and his whispers to you.

We live in such a busy world filled with unnecessary noise that hinders God's loving voice. As we journey with Jesus and carry our cross, we should make every effort to stop, and sit to hear God. He speaks to us much, yet we allow this world to become louder than his voice we carry within, through the Holy Spirit.

God truly desires all of your attention and to do that we need to be centered and focused on him. That is how we allow the whispers to flow deeply within our hearts.

May you hear much of his plans for you, while you relax your mind. Allow Jesus to take your plans in his hands and unfold what all he has in store for you while you simply be still and hear. God holds the door open, it is up to us to enter and surrender to solitude with him. We then can take part in his everyday plans and truly hear as he whispers in our ears.

May we sit and hear the whispers as we direct our focus towards our Lord and Savior Jesus Christ daily.

WHISPERS FROM JESUS

*John 10:3
The gatekeeper opens the gate for him, and the sheep listen to his voice. He calls his own sheep by name and leads them out.*

WHISPERS FROM JESUS

Come rest in Jesus, while you enjoy loving whispers of peace, hope and serenity. Truly a beautiful experience that comes from spending time with Jesus so you can flourish and prepare for all he has planned for you.

Time with Jesus has been precious, such a gift, with such beautiful whispers to hear.

Matthew 10:27
What I tell you in the dark, speak in the daylight; what is whispered in your ear, proclaim from the roofs.

WHISPERS FROM JESUS

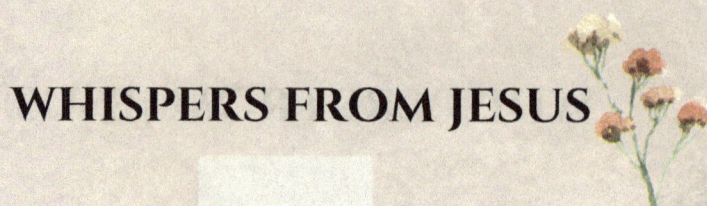

Child you mustn't forget the words I have laid out so freely in my name, don't forget to stop and take a look.

WHISPERS FROM JESUS
DAY 1

My children tend to ask before they truly experience and know me—how to know if God really exists? Well, its truly simple. Seek to know me and you will find me. I will reveal much of my presence, if you take the time to spend with me.

My children are running away without realizing it. It is I who keeps them safe through it all, awaiting their return and finally, the understanding of their need for me.

1 John 5:1

WHISPERS FROM JESUS
DAY 2

Through solitude you can
truly experience my voice, may you find
the deep silence I allow within.
Quiet your mind for me.
My children feel alone, yet wouldn't, if
they'd just come to me. I need your direct
attention here on me but you must
come to me to understand.
Seek complete solitude with me, as worldly
distractions disturb all the whispers I allow
to flow in your heart, mind and soul.

Sit still with me, to learn all I have in store
for you.
Let my whispers guide your feet.
Stand firm in trusting God through faith,
belief and steadfastness.

Romans 8:38-39;
1 Corinthians 15:58

WHISPERS FROM JESUS
DAY 3

Stay hopeful as with God, your future is promising. Where God is, fear cannot exist, so we then get to explore life.
With purpose in mind for the Glory Of God.

How can we not be excited for such an opportunity.

Now let us sit and relax through the whispers so we can follow Christ and experience the journey he called us to be on.

Isaiah 58:11;
Psalm 71:14-16

WHISPERS FROM JESUS
DAY 4

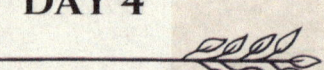

I see you look all around, truly searching for me, then return to feeling lonely. There's no need for this child take a look deep within.

That's where you can find me. So continue to sit with me and read my word, drink of my water, and feed yourself through me. That is exactly where you can find me.

1 Peter 5:7;
Luke 4:4

WHISPERS FROM JESUS
DAY 5

I collect each and every tear. Here let me wipe your worries away while you pick up my word and just read for a moment with me. This is where my children can find much peace.

Jesus will bring comfort
no matter how bad things seem
he makes a way because he
is the way.

And remember if you ever need help
rising again my hand is readily available
to you always.
Cling to me.

Isaiah 41:10;
Deuteronomy 10:20-21

WHISPERS FROM JESUS
DAY 6

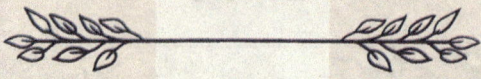

Child never forget all that I am and all I can do.

Your situation can change in a moment.

There is nothing that will ever outweigh my great help or love for you.

Jeremiah 31:3

WHISPERS FROM JESUS
DAY 7

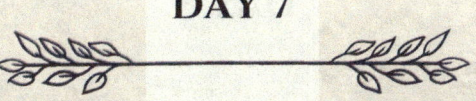

Hold your hands up to the heavens and grab my hand. Take me along with you wherever you go. I will keep you safe and you'll never have to be alone.

What you are experiencing today will soon be but a memory and you shall know it was me. You are going to be ok, keep me close and you'll always be safe.

Philippians 4:13;
Ephesians 3:19

WHISPERS FROM JESUS
DAY 8

I know your worries and fears, and I have overcome all of it from the beginning. Here, leave it all with me because I need your feet to keep moving as you follow me, we have a plan and purpose to meet, and we are not to be defeated before you reach your destiny. If you walk alongside me, I can assure you your doubts and worries won't matter eventually. When you see what I have laid out for you, you will recall the way you took to get there. So keep following this path with me.

Matthew 16:24-26

WHISPERS FROM JESUS
DAY 9

Many of my children do not understand they can simply sit with me to hear and know my plans.
To release your struggles and pain, hand it over, and sit here with me instead of in your head.

The flesh is deceiving and can be such a difficult thing to overcome, much less how all the burdens can make you feel. But you know there is
such a great plan throughout it all with me. And you child will see right through the flames as I go before you increasing your sight.

Psalm 32:8

WHISPERS FROM JESUS
DAY 10

It is I who walks with you throughout the darkness, who simply blows out the flames as you walk through the fires.

Lighting you up for all to see I do exist through my people. To reach your purpose through me should always be the priority. No one can steal it from you, you must hold it close in your heart or you can lose it along the way. This walk will require much faith and strength, but it is I who will sustain you.

John 8:12

WHISPERS FROM JESUS
DAY 11

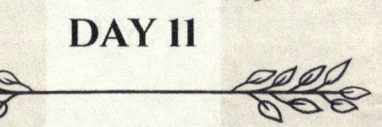

What a sweet thing it is to spread love. Did you know that I will never allow anyone to steal my love for you, if you ever feel as though you've lost it just know the devil is a liar and that's not ever from God.

My love leads, it carries, it heals. The love I allow in your heart holds such peace and healing for you and others. So make sure you spread love, because wherever you are—I am. And I bring love and forgiveness always.

1 John 4:9-10

WHISPERS FROM JESUS
DAY 12

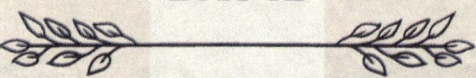

This road could become unsteady and difficult for my children. As you weren't called for life not to happen but for it to happen alongside God.

Remember we are trampling over the darkness in this world. Overcoming it all through Christ Jesus. At times my children usually stop their walk, some even fall, realizing they are slightly lost. When they recall they forgot to keep their eye on me by my word, and following me. With the trials and pain, they became weary and tired noticing themselves walking along with no armor on, no guide because they placed their problem before me.

What will my children learn, teach and say if they never had to lean on me everyday? The purpose and call to your plan is in my hands. So let me take the lead.

Romans 8:18
Luke 11:28

WHISPERS FROM JESUS
DAY 13

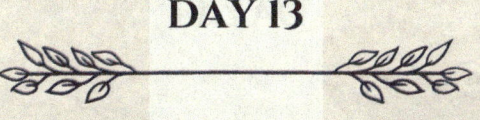

I wish you could see yourself through my eyes, the way I see you. It would surely make you smile. Child, you were created beautifully through me and let no man tell you differently. I was intentional regarding every part of you, accept my work and marvelous creation in each and every child.

Psalm 139: 13-14 (nKJv)
For you formed my inward parts; You covered me in my mother's womb. I will praise you, for I am fearfully and wonderfully made; Marvelous are your works, and that my soul knows very well.

WHISPERS FROM JESUS
DAY 14

What is love, child you ask?
Love is found here with me, Jesus is love.
Some of my children grow up feeling unloved,
alone, some parent-less, some never hugged.

Yet when they find me, they seem to think
they need it physically. What they don't
understand is that the love they are seeking
regardless of all who can come into their lives
will never compare to the love of Jesus.

And if my children don't find it they
keep seeking in a world that truly
cannot carry the love they need.

No need to search any longer with me,
child. I am here and trust that I will
provide all the love you could ever
need.

Psalm 27:10
Romans 5:8

WHISPERS FROM JESUS
DAY 15

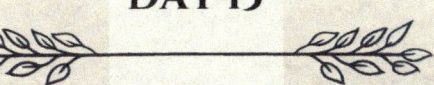

Sit here with me a while. The world steals time, and I return it. By investing time with me, your days are much more productive. My children place so much energy in worrying and wondering, yet I make the days easy when you make time for me. So come to me. Focusing on the obstacles will flourish them, and focusing on me will flourish you. So stay planted and sturdy in my soil instead. It's good and safe ground. Out of it sprouts many flowers with petals that do not wilt, as I hold you strong in firm ground.

Galatians 6:9
Ephesians 4:15

WHISPERS FROM JESUS
DAY 16

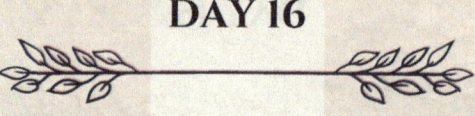

You question if you are enough and ask the ones who make you feel less than but you haven't asked me. I am God, your creator and considering all that I am—to create one such as you I think that tells you enough.

Your plan and purpose through me will absolutely show those who treat you less than you are a part of my big plan. And hopefully one day through you they will no longer treat others less than and know they can follow me too. I intentionally showed them all you are because you are my child. You are becoming all I intended you to be because you chose to place your heart and trust in my hands. But know they do not know or trust me, and that all my children they treat so badly will always succeed with me.

Romans 8:28

WHISPERS FROM JESUS
DAY 17

Some say I am no where to be found, but they are usually the ones who prayed and left. Not waiting for me to respond. Not truly asking and believing with their whole heart. How could one truly come to know me if they don't wait for me to show up for them.

The world is so quick to judge or says a prayer, leave me and think it's done, but what can faith without works become? They must take a seat longer and wait with me, repent and believe, that's when the whispers and answers come easily. They will see my mighty hand of help if they wail on their knees and wait on me.

Psalm 130:5
Psalm 142:1

WHISPERS FROM JESUS
DAY 18

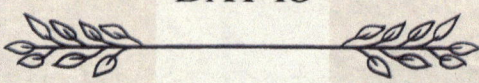

Remember when this world becomes too much, that I Jesus am enough. I have conquered and overcome the world; it has been finished and accomplished for you.
Trust me, not this world.
Follow me and not man.

Ask and you shall receive your request by your faith.
Repent.
Accept my healing.
Knock and my door will open.
Reach out and I will hold you.
Take hold of my words and keep them as I will keep you.

Let my whispers speak louder than the world.

Romans 10:11

WHISPERS FROM JESUS
DAY 19

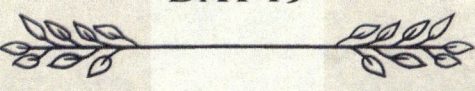

Faith may be difficult due to mans fleshly ways, as I am not visible. If you sit still enough in my presence you will hear the whispers I send to your thoughts as you listen closely.

The whispers most say they cannot hear, yet don't take a moment to wait with me.

Let your heart hear, open my word, open your hearts and ears. It is then you should hear.

2 Corinthians 5:7
For we live by faith, not by sight.

Hebrews 11:6

WHISPERS FROM JESUS
DAY 20

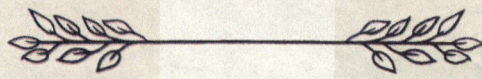

Sit with me, I promise you will hear my words speaking directly to your heart. You will know it's something you never would have said, thought of or imagined. And this is for some how faith may begin.
When the whispers continue to speak through the Holy Spirit for me.

And although I am always
with you, you will start to navigate life knowing for a fact I am beside you, and this is what allows your faith to bloom.

Hebrews 11:1
Proverbs 4:20-22

Romans 10:17
So then faith comes by hearing, and hearing by the word of God.

WHISPERS FROM JESUS
DAY 21

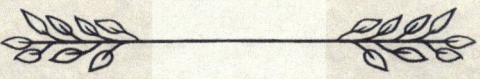

My children get lost in a world full of noise, people and things, yet it shows no love. People, places and things will never save my children. Yet they trust the world and believe what someone mutters in hate, but you can't believe what I whisper in love?

This world is corrupt. Open your eyes child. If you sit and sulk in what they say, how will you allow my love to step in.

Let the Holy Spirit work by considering me instead. When the world speaks badly about my children, this is not of me. So I whisper over and over again, please hear me instead.

Romans 12:2

WHISPERS FROM JESUS
DAY 22

I see you worrying in fear about tomorrow,
yet all you have is today right here, right
now, dear child. Let's focus on what can
be done as of now.

Keep your focus on me.

Do you really think there is
anything too big for me?
Come read and pray with me.
I will be waiting, worrying is such a waste.
Simply spending time with me can
preserve your time, energy, day and life.

Come tell me your worries, sit and pray
that is all you need to do,
and I will take care of the "rest"
for you.

Jeremiah 32:17
Matthew 6:27

WHISPERS FROM JESUS
DAY 23

I know your pain, but I also know my plan. Wait for it, child. Hope in me.

Job 35:14

WHISPERS FROM JESUS
DAY 24

Dear child, I desire for
you to hear and know me.
Look up, rest and feel the warmth of your breath
while you experience my presence
within as I am with you.

As long as you are striving to
follow my plan you need not worry.
You are more than enough.
Never let anyone steal your
worth in me.

<u>A Prayer for you</u>
Dear child, I pray you see you
as I do. Remember I knew you before
anyone else. I knitted all of you in your mothers
womb. My work is perfect, and my people
beautiful.
Take another look at yourself, I pray you
begin to see yourself as I do.
Amen.

Psalm 139:13-14

WHISPERS FROM JESUS
DAY 25

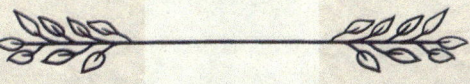

That blessing and prayer
you long and wait for,
trust me is worth all
the waiting.

You will see.

It all has been
planned out perfectly for you.

All you have to do
is stay with me.

The gift of my promises awaits
as so should
you.

Isaiah 30:18

WHISPERS FROM JESUS
DAY 26

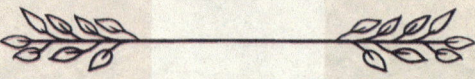

I hear each and every prayer my children say and I too want to bless many, yet it is a process and my timing precise. I ask for patience dear child.
Patience is a gift, and difficult to acquire.

Most do not wait, walking away too soon before their blessing or answered prayer takes place. Then wonder where I went, yet they left it.

The belief was not there, I need my children close to hear so it all can take place.

Lamentations 3:25

WHISPERS FROM JESUS
DAY 27

Child,
don't start your day without me.
Remember me always, and do not allow
yourself to become self-sufficient; start
each day with me.
Keep me near always. As with me
you will know exactly how to conquer all
that occurs each day in a better way.

If you don't place me first, self will get in
the way causing many falls along the way.
I consider brave those who take
this path and choose me as the way. Most
don't because they think it is too much of
a task, but this life can become too much
without me.

2 Timothy 2:3
John 15:4-5

WHISPERS FROM JESUS
DAY 28

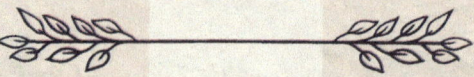

When you awaken, pray.
Don't forget who breathes life
into you each day.

Thank God for another
day, always.

Another day, another opportunity
to grow closer with me.
Living for me and my plan
for you is the ultimate goal.

When we choose God's way,
there's a protection in all we do
each day.
So don't forget about me today.

Psalm 90:14

Matthew 6:9-13

WHISPERS FROM JESUS
DAY 29

You child are so incredibly special to me, I know your heart yearns to reach all of your goals and dreams, and that I love.

What you must know is I sent all my children here with a purpose and plan.

I will guide you to it, however in order for it to take place there are steps to take with me along the way, otherwise there will be delays. Lay all your worries and fears down, quit trusting self for your plans and trust in me. Let me handle the way of your future.

Jeremiah 29:11

WHISPERS FROM JESUS
DAY 30

When you pray, don't just pray and walk away. Sit with me. Open your bible to see what words you may need. May you find comfort and seal your prayers and answers from me, perhaps? There is much to learn with me in the waiting. Most of my children pray, walk away and it is done? Yes, faith can be enough, yet some lack belief for it to become. They hesitate thinking already they aren't heard or won't receive the help they need, yet did not sit with me enough to know I am God, and with me it is finished. Belief is the key, but I am not here for give and take, when you pray make sure you believe in my great works and know that I love you. Spread your belief in my faithfulness through thanksgiving, gratitude, praise, and worship. Stay with me learning through every moment as you wait with me, may you start to see your prayers answered some slowly, some quickly, but the waiting is worth every moment you may spend in the secret place with me.

Matthew 6:6-7
Jeremiah 33:3

WHISPERS FROM JESUS
DAY 31

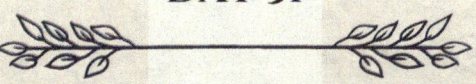

I watch as my children will spend
a lifetime searching for love, yet I am love. I am
with them, and they don't stop to see me.

I am here awaiting patiently from above.
My love for you is more than
the billions on the earth.

The world doesn't compare, it's a true love that
will never leave. The love you've lacked
and lost. You child were created by my hands, out of
my love for you.

But the world comes and
steals you away.

I stay longing for all to find me.
I poured my heart out to you, and
gave up everything on the cross
for your salvation and to truly experience my fathers
love.

John 15:9-13

WHISPERS FROM JESUS
DAY 32

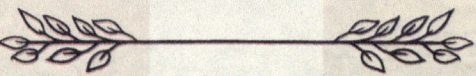

Where is the silence in this world.
If my children would stop for a
moment, and learn to be still. They
could truly know me and my love.

There is no silence around, and
deafened ears to my sound. Due to
the enemy shouting loud always.
However, those who stop to hear
me, will hear.
Many I call but surrounded by
the world they cannot hear
or know me.

When its simple to
come sit and listen
for me.

Keep your ears open,
and your heart growing by
seeking me.

Psalm 46:10

WHISPERS FROM JESUS
DAY 33

My children truly yearn to know and hear me, which is such a gift and joy for me to see.

However, the mind can be deceptive.
I see it time after time.
My children born of the spirit,
yet the enemy finds every opportunity to steal the gifts I have freely given, so be cautious of this.

Ask yourself, is this of God, or fear.
And recall anything from God
will not cause you to be filled with fear or bad thoughts. Something wants to stop your journey of truly experiencing me.

Quiet your minds and hear my whispers loudly, sit, meditate and pray to hear me

Philippians 4:7;
Proverbs 4:23

WHISPERS FROM JESUS
DAY 34

Let us take a moment to pray:

Dear Father God,
Thank you for allowing me another
day, may I remember to choose your
will and way with all I do today.

Lord, help me walk closely with you, guide my
feet and show me all you need me to do.

Help me to take a seat with you and plant
myself into your word so that I may grow and
keep your word rooted deep within my soul.
I pray for me to have faith in you to succeed.
A mustard seed is all I need.
Thank you Lord Jesus for all you have done for
me and many.
In Jesus' mighty name, I pray. Amen.
Thank you God.

Hebrews 10:22-23

WHISPERS FROM JESUS
DAY 35

Dear Father God,

I come to you and place my worries
in your hands.
Lord help me to know
without you I am not able to follow
your great plans for me, and Lord,
I so eagerly yearn to.

Keep my heart safe, my mind pure full of
love in your hands, as I know
at any moment things of this world will
happen yet I know who holds my plan,
and I must keep my heart pure focused
on you.

In Jesus' Might name, I pray. Amen.
I praise you, Jesus.

Matthew 5:8

**WHISPERS FROM JESUS
DAY 36**

I see you child, coming back to me, keep coming back, I don't expect perfection I expect you.

ISAIAH 55:11

Matthew 19:26 (nKJv)
But Jesus looked at them and said to them,
"With men this is impossible, but with God
all things are possible."

WHISPERS FROM JESUS
DAY 37

I know you can't see me,
but that doesn't mean
you can't experience me.

If all things lovely were seen,
what hope would you have? How would
it be inspiring that faith alone can bring
me alive in those who believe.

Wonder and expectation truly makes me
known and speaks through those who
seek to know me.

The belief and knowing me personally is
everything, faith in knowing who I am
without seeing
is key to truly experiencing me.

John 20:28-29

WHISPERS FROM JESUS
DAY 38

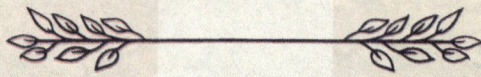

Why do you feel it is you who can control the
outcomes in life, dear child?
How is it worry will create the best outcome?
Consider this during these times,
I am the only one that can truly
control, guide and protect the outcome.
Not fear and worrying, this could worsen
your outcomes.

I see you doing this and doing that. Walking
around in distress, when simply all you need to
do is come to me. Let us join in prayer and
belief so that I your heavenly Father can bring
forth the correct solutions you will need.
Place your worries in my hands.
If the problem seems too big, you
must remember me. Now stop, sit and listen
for me. My whispers of the way are there but
you are too busy fretting to hear.

Philippians 4:6-7

WHISPERS FROM JESUS
DAY 39

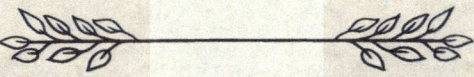

Dear child, thank you for sitting with me. I know you can't see it now, but this path with me can be easier, if you let me handle the difficulties. Stay, and you'll see the days become brighter with hope and expectation of me. The light will shine bright, you will no longer sit in the darkness with the heavy weight of the world.

You will rise as the sun does and be the light throughout darkness. Allow me to guide the way, and you will see my light regardless of the time of day.

Matthew 5:16
2 Samuel 22:29-31

WHISPERS FROM JESUS
DAY 40

Child, don't let life steal the heart I gave you. Guard yourself with me. I am truly here to help you. I have overcome this world and can overcome all trials you may face. You need not worry with me.

Such a simple task to understand and know your life has always been in my hands, yet my children let go because they can't simply grasp this. Yet they take a-hold of everything else. That is how you will find me, a relationship—communicate, sit, be still and listen.
This is painless, yet rarely accomplished. Please hear me. And watch. Watch how much easier life flows by sitting and handing each and every worry over to me.

Proverbs 3:5-6
Jeremiah 32:17

WHISPERS FROM JESUS
DAY 41

Oh dear child, I see you.
I see all you have been through
come to me. Rest here in my
arms, while I tend to you.
You don't have to do a thing right
now, allow me to show you the way.

While you trust and have faith in me.
Relax your mind through me,
that is my request.
Matthew 7:7

Psalm 37:7 (nKJv)
Rest in the Lord, and wait patiently
for Him; Do not fret because of him
who prospers in his way, Because of
the man who brings wicked schemes
to pass.

WHISPERS FROM JESUS
DAY 42

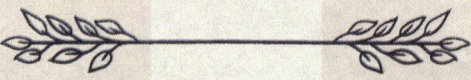

With me child, fear cannot live.
When fear arises, ask yourself this:
Do you truly trust me or the lies
of the enemy?

I know it is easy to
forget all I can do for you or you may
think I do not hear you, but oh, dear child, I
hear. And the thoughts of this or that to allow
fear are never of me.

Don't let the enemies loud voice
overcome mine. I may whisper but the peace it
allows far outweighs the screaming and shouting
he loves to create causing my children to fear.

And when you pray, please know everything is
a process in my great works and my timing is
always perfect if you allow it. Wait on the Lord.

Isaiah 40:31
Revelation 3:10-11

WHISPERS FROM JESUS
DAY 43

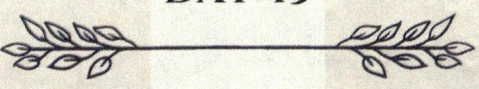

I love you child, don't forget that.
I made you perfectly for my glory pay no attention to what the world says.

Listen to what I say about you. I made you intentionally, I make no mistakes, so please love all I created you to be.

Because in my eyes you are perfect to me.

Isaiah 2:22

WHISPERS FROM JESUS
DAY 44

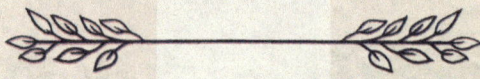

If you fall, I will always catch you, if you let me. However, many times unknowingly I have carried you.

Put your focus towards my goal and you will not fail as I have laid out the plan.

I just need you to follow and stay close to me so you know exactly what steps to take. Remember it is I who can strengthen you for the climb.

I see my dear children struggle with simply allowing me to take over, making each task more difficult than it needs to be.
How can you follow if you do not let go and focus on walking my way and trusting me?

Jeremiah 17:23

Philippians 4:13

WHISPERS FROM JESUS
DAY 45

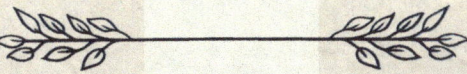

Oh, what little faith I see in this world.
I hear the shouts of, "God doesn't hear me!"
This world does not compare to my great works.
Do not look out in despair, direct your attention to me. You will see I am already there and in the midst of everything you are being directed to my plan for your life.
Don't give up. Let me carry you along.

And I will show you all I can provide by you just allowing me in and staying close to me. Will it ever be instant, sometimes, but not always. Good things and great gifts take time and preparation.
How do we keep those gifts? By all you learn in the waiting.

When you gift someone do you just simply hand it over as is—unwrapped, not cared for with love?
You would handle it with great care, concern, time and effort so it truly matters when it is gifted to the recipient. Know that your loving father gifts in a similar way too.

Ephesians 3:20

WHISPERS FROM JESUS
DAY 46

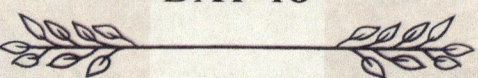

Don't disappear on me. I know it
seems you are waiting and waiting, but know
that your waiting and suffering with me is
never wasted.
You are on your way with patience and
perseverance, although you may not see
all that may be going on behind the scenes.
The preparation during the wait will lead your
way. The issue my children have difficulty with
is no one wants to be patient with me.
Yet am I not patient with you?

My child, if you only knew
all I had planned. It saddens me
that I can be on the verge of gifting
and blessing my children, then they flee away
from me. How can I answer and work on your
behalf if you have gone astray.

Romans 8:18
Psalm 126:5

WHISPERS FROM JESUS
DAY 47

Stay awhile, it
is best to be here with me, rather
than seeking worldly things that will
quickly slip away and are short lived. Seek first
the kingdom of God, as my love is everlasting
and will not fail. Once you truly understand
this and my great works, you will want to be
no where other than with me.

In my hands, comforted,
experiencing a peace and joy
the world and things will
never provide.
More beautiful than any
material gift you can find.

With me is where life and love begins, worries
fade, and my Glory reigns.

Isaiah 49:16
Psalm 139:10

WHISPERS FROM JESUS
DAY 48

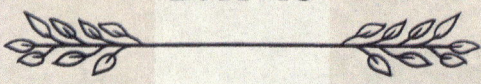

Take advantage of these sweet moments with me in your secret place.
The whispers come freely, and peace isn't something my children seek through me—yet I provide it so freely.

I believe the concept of time and sitting still with me is beyond their fleshly understanding. Something so simple they cannot fathom, yet if they did, they would experience much peace.

Romans 5:1 (NIV)
Therefore, since we have been justified through faith,
we have peace with God through our Lord
Jesus Christ

WHISPERS FROM JESUS
DAY 49

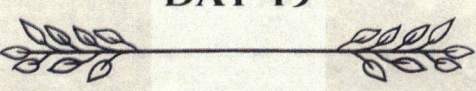

What will time with me cost you? Nothing.

What will you gain from time with me?
EVERYTHING.

I will provide ALL you need to succeed. FOR MY PURPOSE, HOPE and a future of TRUE PEACE.

"For I know the plans I have for you,' declares the Lord, 'plans to prosper you and not to harm you, plans to give you a hope and a future."
Jeremiah 29:11 (NIV)

WHISPERS FROM JESUS
DAY 50

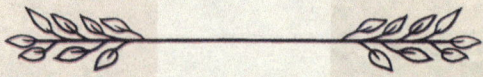

Don't walk around sad. Joy shows the hand of God upon you. So choose JOY regardless of what those around you do or the trials you face.
And remember child your circumstances do not define your presence through me. Carry me with you every moment. I will exude light and happiness through you to encourage many for my Glory. I didn't call my children to be sad in the flesh but to rejoice in me. As with me sadness cannot linger.

Hear my whispers daily for all I have in store for you, so you have hope for today and others you meet along the way. Walking in hope that one day they may also want to sit and feed their souls with me.

2 Timothy 2:1
James 1:2-4

WHISPERS FROM JESUS
DAY 51

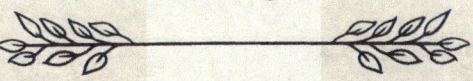

The longing I understand, I long for my children to stop and wait with me.
Just as you long for your prayer to be answered I long for you trust in me.

Believe and wait as I know you so badly want to be taken out of your situation, but if you know me—who I am, I am with you within, and I understand.

I will answer you when you call out with your whole heart. So do not fear for I am near.

Psalm 34:17

WHISPERS FROM JESUS
DAY 52

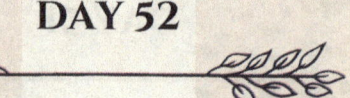

Come to me, quiet your mind and be still. Ask me anything if you need to, sit in your secret place and you shall hear my whispers within.
Breathe my life within you in, while you exhale to release all of your worries.

Practicing stillness with me allows your ears to hear me while living in a world so full of noise.
So that eventually when you go out in the world daily, you continue to carry the silence and stillness within. While you hear the whispers from me and speak from the Holy Spirit within to others.

1 Kings 19:11-13

WHISPERS FROM JESUS
DAY 53

Breathe, relax and
just be here with me.

Open my word and there you
will find all the answers to
your worries directly from me.

AND REMEMBER WHEN YOU
THINK IT CAN'T BE DONE,
GOD CAN DO IT.

All it takes is commitment, a
deep rooted relationship with
me, repentance, faith, belief
and hearing.

Proverbs 16:3

WHISPERS FROM JESUS
DAY 54

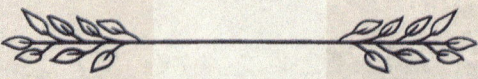

My child, your help comes from me. And me alone. At times my children will search and search, feeding their souls with people and stuff they think will provide love. Yet deepening the emptiness and leaving you in despair because the people and material things in this world will never provide the love your heart needs.

We live in a world seeking, yet not knowing the true love of Jesus.

With me you are fully loved and protected. The biggest lie the enemy tells my children is that I am not there, yet, I have always been present. My children must be present to know and hear me.

1 John 4:7-8
Psalm 121:2-3

WHISPERS FROM JESUS
DAY 55

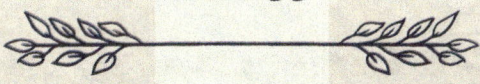

I know all of your struggles, and can offer the help you need. Therefore, the best place to run is to me. At times that's how my children find me. Through situations they know with all their heart, nothing or no one else can fix.

Through complete loneliness and solitude, they must finally sit and seek me.

Your prayers are heard even if you can't see what I am doing, know nothing goes unheard by me.

Psalm 25:14-18
Isaiah 41:13

WHISPERS FROM JESUS
DAY 56

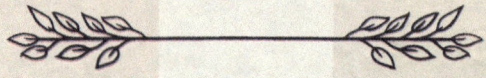

Take a step outside child, notice my creations. And look above, just reflect on me, who I am and all I can do if you surround yourself with me. Feel my presence as you view the plants, the grass, the flowers and warm glistening sun or even the clouds.

Pray and think of me, listen for the sweet sounds of my voice that truly comes in whispers to your heart and soul.

Let the air of my creations breathe life upon you.
And allow my whispers to speak louder than the enemy.

Psalm 146:1-3

WHISPERS FROM JESUS
DAY 57

<u>Let us pray:</u>

Dear God, we thank you Lord.
We thank you for your goodness upon us. For your hand over us, and your loving care and concern. Your mercy and everlasting love never ceases to amaze us.

Through every season you hear us.
You await your child's call so graciously. Tending to our prayers and cries with great help in your perfect timing. All while we wait and learn of your great works patiently.

Lord, we could never thank you enough for such blessings. We pray to hear all the beautiful whispers you place in our ears.
In Jesus' mighty name, we pray.
Amen.

Psalm 61:1-3;
Jeremiah 29:12-13

WHISPERS FROM JESUS
DAY 58

Be cautious, pray and seek me through everything.

This world is full of misery due to disobedience and those not truly knowing me. It needs my love, and for those in this world to seek and live through me then the misery and hatred would flee.

In the meantime while we wait for the others, we work together.
Which encourages you to share my love and all I am capable of doing with others. And through you they may find me.

If only my children would come to me, they'd find love and peace internally. All they so desperately seek but can't find because they don't know me. Sometimes I must call and call and shut doors until they finally hear me. Then they know those whispers they once heard were truly a gift from me.

Romans 13:10
Lamentations 3:25

WHISPERS FROM JESUS
DAY 59

Open your bible, seek a verse
that resonates with you. And
sit quietly with me.

Here you'll find much comfort and peace
by with my words.

May your journey begin simple, and I hope
here is where you'll stay.

So you can start to seek me
easily each new day.

When my children come and truly seek me
from the depths of their hearts; that's when
I can start to mold you into the person you
were created to be, you don't have to
come perfectly.

Isaiah 64:8

WHISPERS FROM JESUS
DAY 60

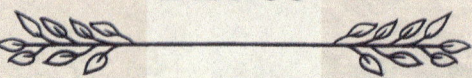

Child, here, set it down.
Lay it all in my hands.
Allow me to take over all of your burdens. As you trying to carry it all can be heavy.
Let it go, give it to me.
I need you on this walk with me, and I can't have anything weighing you down as I have a very specific plan.

May your walk with me be strengthened as you rest at ease now that you have handed it over to me.

Psalm 55:22 (nKJv)
Cast your cares on the LORD
and he will sustain you;
he will never let the
righteous be shaken.

WHISPERS FROM JESUS
DAY 61

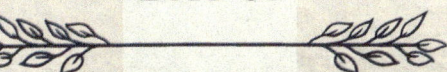

Hear my whispers from heaven to you.
If you feel as if you are unable to hear me some-days,
open my word and pray in
your secret place.
Pray for your ears to hear, quiet your mind and place
yourself away from everything.
Even if it's just for a moment.

It may seem like it won't help, but the flesh can make you think in this way. Be cautious of this very thing, it can cause you take a step back due to lack of time or needing to take care of everything. However, there is no need to worry about that as I will allow you the time you need by multiplying the time back for time spent with me.

And the simplicity can appear difficult to many, yet through time with me you will hear and experience many things that will allow you to rejoice and feel me surround your entire being.

I Thessalonians 5:17

WHISPERS FROM JESUS
DAY 62

I will provide all you need to
continue throughout the battles, you don't
go alone when you stay close to me.

Remember to come to me and
carry me with you. Rest at ease in my care.

How you ask? By beginning each new day
with me, at times every moment and every
interaction.

Pray, ask, believe and receive
my help. Many will wonder how you
experience much alone but what
they may not understand is you
are never alone with me. As you my child
invite me in and they can too as
well.

James 4:8
John 10:28

WHISPERS FROM JESUS
DAY 63

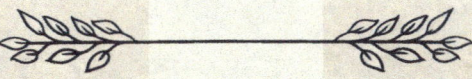

Go out and smile and live out my grace.
The grace I have allowed you, share it with others.

Love others even when they don't love you, that is the beginning of my spirit and love
flowing through you.
Carry it along with you, leaning on me to guide you. As some will question how is it
you are still kind throughout your trials. They can find me through this very experience with you. This is also how others may experience my love, through my children.

As we all know the flesh loves to be full of unforgiveness and sadness but the father is not.

God has already forgiven and loved us.
With him it has been finished, accomplished and done. Let us remind ourselves of how much the father loved us that he gave his only son
for our sins to be forgiven.

Matthew 6:14

WHISPERS FROM JESUS
DAY 64

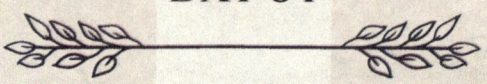

Let us pray:

Dear God, thank you for reminding me daily of your great love and protection. Lord, I pray you may strengthen me for this walk. That no matter what may come, I will choose you.

Thank you Jesus for your whispers to me, help me to take moments to stop and hear you, and not me.

Help me stay traveling this road to your purpose for me and I pray I not lose sight of you and where you need me to go. Amen.

Proverbs 20:24

WHISPERS FROM JESUS
DAY 65

I created this world, but not only
that, I created YOU.
And I did so meticulously
Why? Because I loved and knew you
before you were created. I brought you here
to live for and through me. And not for and through
this world.
It's a decision my children have the opportunity to
make. Live for the world or for Jesus who has
overcome the world and all of your sins on
the cross. To some this may seem like an easy
choice to make.
Yet the enemy shouts, "choose me, pick me, I'll
give you this and that, riches and fame,
all the feel good stuff". The things that will never
remain the way Jesus does because all of his gifts
are a lifetime of love, protection, forgiveness and
eternity above, not anything you could buy or receive
here on earth. There is no price tag or shiny material
things that could ever show love like Jesus does.

John 3:27

Romans 11:36

WHISPERS FROM JESUS
DAY 66

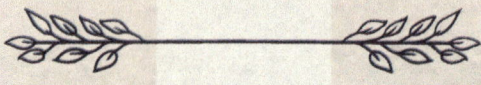

I've watched my children, and see they want it right now because it feels good for a moment and in their closed off hearts they know that.
Or pray for things and go on as if they don't need to trust me.

Then run off to the next thing.
But what happens when all of the earthly things and wants run out?
What's next?
They are left with an empty world, full of insufficiency if they don't have or keep me close.

As they chose things that
were temporary, yet Jesus is eternal, and his love and help endless.

Matthew 8:26

WHISPERS FROM JESUS
DAY 67

Ephesians 1:11

It may feel as if every
attempt of your work
for me fails. Every time you
turn there may be a new obstacle
or problem ahead, but child
you must remember
regardless of setbacks
I hold the plan.

As long as you are following me,
attempting to accomplish what I
have set out for you, my will for you
will be done.

*Let the father guide you
to it and through it.*

WHISPERS FROM JESUS
DAY 68

Hope in Jesus.
Trust his plan, child.
For God knows the plan for
your life. For your good.
I will be with you now
and forever.

But let me be the guide.
Psalm 119:114

Psalm 27:14 (nKJv)
Wait on the Lord; be of
Be of good courage, and
he will strengthen your
heart; wait, I say,
on the Lord.

WHISPERS FROM JESUS
DAY 69

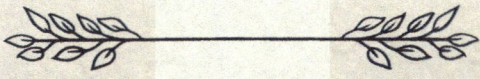

I see your tears, and know your fears.
But did you know with me I will wipe all of it
away. Although you may experience
it, your joy will come in the waiting.

A peace and joy that is beyond human
comprehension. So while you feel as
though you are waiting for ever. Just know
nothing good ever comes without a wait.
Ask yourself what good can come from
something quickly handed over, it must be
molded and formed for protection. Don't
let your flesh disrupt something
being made so beautifully.

What may look inconvenient
now could be the blessing you
need, made perfectly.

2 Corinthians 9:8-10

WHISPERS FROM JESUS
DAY 70

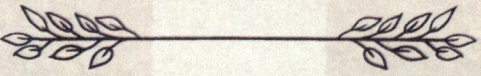

Keep your hope in me.
Lay your heart to rest in
my hands and let the joy and
fullness begin, as you become whole
with me.
Experience the peace I set inside
you from just allowing me
to take over your entire being.

Something so many miss as they walk
away and say I am no where
to be found. Yet they did not
call out to me or hope and believe in
me and all I had in store for them.

Romans 15:13;
James 4:8

WHISPERS FROM JESUS
DAY 71

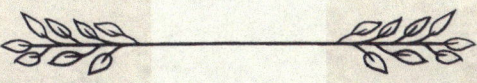

Find joy in my presence, I know it seems so distant to you right now. However, know I see you child, all the trials and pain you feel you can't withstand, just remember this is temporary.

Armor yourself with me, and let me take over from here.

My love for you is forever, seek it and you will walk joyfully with me during all of this.

My presence and Holy Spirit within you changes things. Trust in me throughout it, and watch me work on your behalf.

-Jesus

Romans 12:12

WHISPERS FROM JESUS
DAY 72

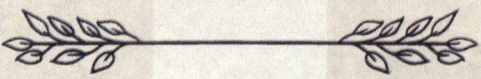

I love my children and want what's best for you.

I know life sometimes seems like such a fight and you may feel depleted and defeated yet you must recall I gave it all for you.

I have not been defeated, I have OVERCOME, as with me you will too.

Choose to keep me close, and together with your faith we will win this. As long as you allow me to have all of your heart, you only need to call on me.

Do not sit in distress too long, I need you to trust me.

Psalm 28:7
James 1:2-4

WHISPERS FROM JESUS
DAY 73

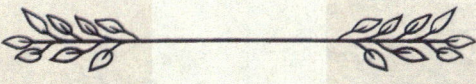

This world runs around breaking my children's hearts.

However, God mends hearts.
You don't have to carry a heart that is separated from me as I see my children do. When your heart breaks enough or even just once, come to me.

Because with me your heart will remain whole as I mold it and hold your life in my hands for a true restoration and healing to take place. Your heart is mine to keep and although you share it with others, you can always bring it back to me to hold and mend.

Stay with me to protect your heart always.

Psalms 34:18

WHISPERS FROM JESUS
DAY 74

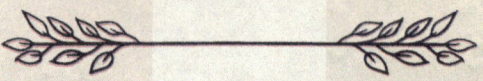

Hope is such a beautiful thing,
don't let the hopeful spirit
I placed in you lose it's place.
Keep it safe by placing your hope in me
along with increasing your faith each
and every day. I will never disappoint
when you place all your trust in me. And
I guarantee you your future will be full
of promises from my father in heaven.

When my children place their life in my
hands, I will always redirect your path
to the most beautiful destiny.
Now this is the love I offer to
those who choose m.

Hebrews 11:1;
Deuteronomy 31:6

WHISPERS FROM JESUS
DAY 75

Oh this life, truly my children will need me throughout all of it. I see many who sit and weep out of loneliness and despair if only they could see I am right there.

Especially in a time of loss and pain, they need me. Reach out and grab my hand to feel that it is me you are lacking.

Make beauty out of this time and the life you were given so freely by me for my purpose. Once that understanding is reached life becomes easier day by day as you're now on a journey for such a purpose and plan for and with me.
Allow me to step in and guide you through and to it.

Your life is precious to me, remember that.

Psalms 16:5
Hebrews 4:16

WHISPERS FROM JESUS
DAY 76

Why is it you call on them, and not me? Why is it you
cry to them. Why is it. I ask my children this.
As your father in heaven, I am questioned
all the time, but where is your trust in me?
Sometimes I feel my children forget I truly do exist.
They wonder why this person can't fix this or do that
or help them in the way they need.
This desperation can lead so many astray,
as it is me they need but they seek and seek to find
more misery.

Child, those you call on are human, and I am
your creator, sustainer, and redeemer.
Yet my children don't call on me. If they did they
would know I can help with a vengeance in all the
ways they need. Providing a plan they could only
dream of. But yet they call on those who truly are
not able to provide what their hearts so badly need.
Be careful where you lay your worries, but I can
assure you all worries are safe in my hands.
Seek me.

2 Corinthians 12:9
2 Samuel 22:33

WHISPERS FROM JESUS
DAY 77

The garden, you are planting with me must be
cared for daily. Watered, loved and full of Jesus.
The more seeds you'll plant if you
allow me to cover your soul daily.
So you can reach a full bloom, don't forget
to shower yourself with me.
Look, imagine your flowers all growing
beautifully. Do you feel the calm these flowers
bring, the peace that surpasses understanding
with each trial that has taken place.

You longed to get here, and you found
serenity. Keep growing with me.

By continuing watch
every part of your being and the seeds
you've planted flourish and grow
through my nourishing.

Your garden will serve as a reminder
of my presence and love.

Song of Solomon 2:12
Philippians 4:7

WHISPERS FROM JESUS
DAY 78

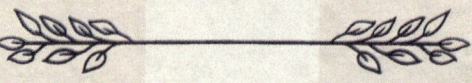

1 Corinthians 3:7

Nourish yourself through
me. Through my
word and our time together
that will truly allow
all my children seek.

Walk diligently
with me and you will have
the path of peace each
step of the way.

Watch the the Holy Spirit
grow throughout you
beautifully.

Stay here with me so you may
hear every whisper
deeper within to
live wonderfully
through me.

WHISPERS FROM JESUS
DAY 79

Call on me, count on me. Be here with me, believe in me. This is my most known plan for you, to know, hear, and experience me.
Most won't stay to hear me.

I am put aside everyday, while distractions take my place, and still my love, help and care for you remains.

You may think I don't need you but if you only knew my plan for you through me. You were placed here for a specific plan for my glory.

Don't wonder lost without me as my children tend to do. Let me lead and guide you.

Psalm 33:20

WHISPERS FROM JESUS
DAY 80

There is always such to gain through my
plan, for my Glory.

If you think deeply about it,
how can you keep my plans
or all that comes your way
inexperienced in the walk
I have for you.

Just like a
baby, they first learn to
crawl, then as they attempt to walk they fall
as they are, "learning."

They weren't born ready to withstand it all. My
children must also learn how to walk with their
cross. And I as your heavenly Father will carry
you until you can withstand this walk,
if you let me.

Isaiah 46:4

WHISPERS FROM JESUS
DAY 81

You matter child.
You especially matter
much to me. Never
question my work in you.

I have designed you
perfectly, and love all
that you are.

Ephesians 2:10
For we are His workmanship, created in Christ Jesus for good works, which God prepared beforehand that we should walk in them.

WHISPERS FROM JESUS
DAY 82

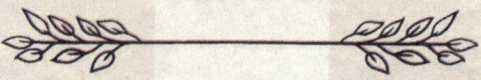

Don't seek love in this world, seek love
through me. Once you find my love
you will know where true love
exist.
My love mends, my love guides, my
love heals, and lives through me and my
children.

Once you find it here with me, then you
carry love with you always.

You will no longer
seek it from humans who will fail you,
things that can be stolen away, and
places you may not always stay.

Love is Jesus, and when you have me, you
can just live through me sharing the love I
so freely placed within
you.

Ephesians 3:19

WHISPERS FROM JESUS
DAY 83

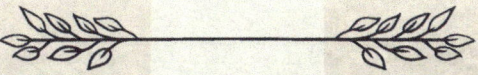

While this world may come against you, don't forget to recall who goes before you. I do.

With me the world is the last place you will seek comfort because my children know the love, peace and comfort I provide.

You may question what is your purpose?
Yet don't stop to recall I sent my people to comfort others through me. But that comfort I provide isn't always easily found in others as they go out to do this or that and not stop to lend my hand. Since I go with you, share me with many that way we can spread love and make the world a much better place for everyone. Your faithful loving walk will always be blessed by me.

2 Corinthians 1:3-4

WHISPERS FROM JESUS
DAY 84

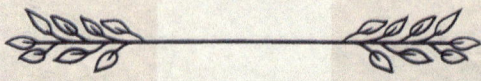

On days when everything seems empty and you can't find meaning, please do not forget about me. Allow me to fill your cup as I will
show you how it overflows with me.
I will guide you to the true meaning through all of it.
Troubles, sorrows and hardships are a part of a bigger and one day—better plan.

Place your life in my hands, regardless of your circumstances it all has meaning. Even if you cannot see it, the breath you breathe,
your life signifies my Glory.

As you travel with me, you will begin
to rest with your entire being
strengthened.

So come and stay close to me.

Matthew 11:28-30
John 8:12

WHISPERS FROM JESUS
DAY 85

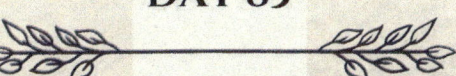

I pray my children stop letting feelings to take over their entire being. If you spend enough time with me, those feeling will turn to joy. Express it all here with me.
What is making
feel sorrowful, through prayer I can help you with? Tell me.

Don't sit in sadness dear child, time is precious.

Find through me the happiness
you may seek and need
for this time you're in.

Keep my love with you,
spread my joy through you
with all whom you meet.

-Jesus

Romans 12:15-18

WHISPERS FROM JESUS
DAY 86

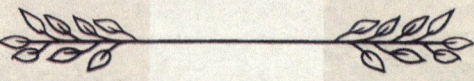

Look to me child,
don't look down, don't look around,
look to me.

Close your
eyes, invite me in and
just be.

Psalms 119:15-18

God is more than
able. Child, choose
Jesus.

My children go running
around choosing many things, but simply
they need to choose
me.

Colossians 3:12-14

WHISPERS FROM JESUS
DAY 87

This life isn't about
the things of the earth, people and
places. I see my children so wrapped
up in this new thing or that. However,
when God is doing a new
thing, they can't see it when the focus is
always on all the things, that truly
will never matter how
Jesus does.

Isaiah 43:18-19

Ephesians 3:20
Now to Him who is able to do exceedingly abundantly above all that we ask or think, according to the power that works in us

WHISPERS FROM JESUS
DAY 88

I see you, please
stay with me. When
you can't find a way,
come and follow me
Because I am the
way.

John 14:6 (nKJv)
*Jesus said to him, "I am the way, the truth,
and the life. No one comes to the Father
except through Me.*

WHISPERS FROM JESUS
DAY 89

Let me lead you.
Hope in me.
Although you don't see
me. Think of when you
hope for a fun day with
a loved one, you envision it, correct?
It makes you smile and hopeful for it.
Keeping you excited
for the day you can experience it.
Place that hope
and expectation in me.

Think of the path of where I will lead, as
you must know with me the destination is
significant and way more profound. While it
may be a difficult journey for a bit, it will be
worth it.

Romans 15:13;
Philippians 4:19

WHISPERS FROM JESUS
DAY 90

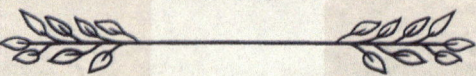

God changes things. I pray you may
lead me Lord Jesus to continue to share
who you are through my troubles and pain.
I will remain joyful throughout my suffering
for your plan for me outweighs it all.
As I know God what healing you will
bring to someone who is in such suffering.
By allowing healing to
others through you, I experience great
healing too.

You are a God of compassion healing, love
and miracles. I pray you may
help me to call out to you any time of day.
Thank you for loving me and my family.

In Jesus's mighty name I pray. Amen.

Lamentations 3:57

WHISPERS FROM JESUS
DAY 91

A Prayer for you:
Dear heavenly father, Lord, I pray you may be with my loved ones and me. This time we are in is not easy, and my cross seems a bit heavy. I recall your suffering for me, and remember this life was not made to be easy, but led by you. Help us lord to stay on track, to continue to follow your path regardless of what happens in life, we will always have you to run to.

In Jesus' name,
I pray. Amen.
Thank you God.

Psalm 46:1

WHISPERS FROM JESUS
DAY 92

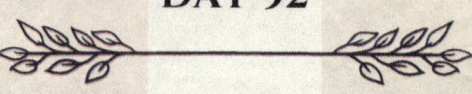

I hear you; I see you,
I am with you.
I go before you.
I am for you.
I believe in you
I have faith in you
I will carry you.
I will hold you
through rough waters
I will shelter you in
my arms.
I will take care of you
in such a mighty way.
Just stay.

2 Samuel 22:30-31

WHISPERS FROM JESUS
DAY 93

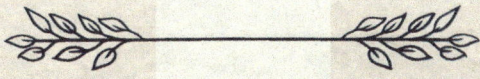

My children come to me, expecting a life with no difficulties. They do good, work hard, they are kind, compassionate. And if I know one thing all I have placed in you child the enemy will take every opportunity to destroy it.

In this world, loss, heartbreak and pain—attacks of the mind, thoughts and character. With me, child, nothing can remove the gifts I hand placed inside of you.

Remember the flesh is weak, yet the Holy Spirit is stronger. Keep me close, filling yourself with the Holy Spirit always. Hear the whispers I place in your heart.

Matthew 26:41

WHISPERS FROM JESUS
DAY 94

Let us pray:

Dear God, thank you for all you do, for your protection over me. Thank you for allowing me breath to live out your will for me.

Father God, allow me the strength and courage I need to follow you and carry out your plan. Be with me every step of the way so I can accomplish all you need me to do. Lord, comfort and hold me through every trial and fleshly pain. May I feel you surround me as I reach out to you, always.

In Jesus' Mighty name I pray Amen.

Psalm 18:1

WHISPERS FROM JESUS
DAY 95

Allow yourself to experience my love for you daily.
I love you more than you can imagine.
I have no desire to witness my children sitting in suffering forgetting all I am able to do.
Traveling closely with me brings all the healing and help you could ever need so do not hesitate to choose me.

I love you. I created you. I knew you before anyone. You were the first of you, my plans and gifts I placed in you, let them be. Simply by recalling my great love and works, and utilizing your personalized gifts I gave to you. Smile as with me your life shall be joyfully lived throughout any experience.

Carry my love with you to share, be a beacon of light through all darkness. For you and others to never wonder lost; as so many do without me.

Luke 1:79

WHISPERS FROM JESUS
DAY 96

My eyes see, and my ears hear you. I hear your
cries from your bedside,
I count the tears left on your pillow.
I place my hand on
your head and say child I am
with you. You sit and wonder,
yet I stand above and strengthen
you.

This you cannot see, just as you cannot see
breath, but you breathe. Allow
yourself to feel surrounded
by me.

Recall the times you
didn't think you'd rise above?
You were rescued by me, exactly what I will do
with each cry out to me.
I see and hear you.

2 Chronicles 7:14
1 John 5:15

WHISPERS FROM JESUS
DAY 97

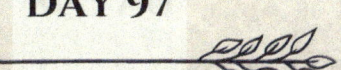

Reach out to me, grab my right hand.
Come and stay
close, safe with me.
I will carry you to safety—places
unseen.
Releasing thoughts only to be known
by me.
Gifts that you would have never
known.
And a peace that overcomes
ALL fleshly understanding.

Do not miss out on these
opportunities so freely provided only
by Jesus.

2 Timothy 1:7;
Jeremiah 33:3

WHISPERS FROM JESUS
DAY 98

Dear child,
send the weight of your troubles to me to
for me to hold and take care of.

My children weren't created
to triumph these battles alone, you were created
to live out my plan through, for and with me—
never alone.

Everything you're fighting for, need or struggling
with it has already been overcome by me so just
trust and believe.

My children need full reliance on me as with self,
the troubles remain. But with faith and my good
works, the results will be such a gift from your
father in heaven. So sit still while I triumph over
every obstacle that comes before and behind
you.

1 Peter 5:7;
Philippians 4:6-7

WHISPERS FROM JESUS
DAY 99

May you not slip and don't hide
due to fear, afraid you will fail. Go out brave and
strong armored by me.

Do not fear a single slip, setback or attack.
Allow me to take over and my children will know
no matter what happens, they are armored
and carried by me.

Your work here may be difficult, yet
fulfilling—a victory with me, I provide such
safety as you suit up armored by me.

In this world hate exist,
but my children go out keeping their lamps full of
oil to allow my light to shine and a love with no
limits. I am incredibly proud of my children who
fight the good fight with me.

Jeremiah 32:17
2 Timothy 4:7

WHISPERS FROM JESUS
DAY 100

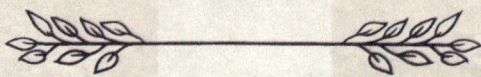

These whispers I have placed here
in your ear.
May you loudly hear.
Don't allow my voice through the Holy Spirit to
become a distant memory. Through time with me
daily, may my whispers remind you of me.

My voice may speak softly, but
why do I need to shout.
So recall my voice through
the stillness and peace with me.
In your heart is where you will
find me.

Sit long enough with me so you
can experience all that I have set out for you.
For I have the answers, hand your burdens
over to me, be still and you shall
hear the whispers from me.

Psalm 139:2;
Revelation 3:10-11

WHISPERS FROM JESUS
From the Author:

Dear Readers,
thank you for being here. I pray this book may reach you, but not just by reading it—I pray for your heart, soul, and mind to hear. Oh, let your heart hear God's plans for you. I pray it exudes how our efforts, time and walk with Jesus are never wasted. And how he will whisper to our hearts and souls if we stop and spend time with him.

If you are a new Christian, I am so incredibly thankful you came to sit with Jesus. He will not fail you; the solitude will be worth it, and far above every voice in this loud world we live in. Jesus doesn't have to scream to get our attention, he simply is. And how we find him is always impactful and well-remembered, yet so quickly we can forget. I pray we recall God's mighty name and help in all that we do so our walk can be of love, promise, compassion and hope to help the next. I pray you will come and sit with Jesus.
Amen.
Thank you, Jesus.

Isaiah 30:21

WHISPERS FROM JESUS

Jesus Loves You

WHISPERS FROM JESUS

Jeremiah 32:17 (NKJV)

Ah, Lord God! Behold, You have made the heavens and the earth by Your great power and outstretched arm. There is nothing too hard for YOU.

WHISPERS FROM JESUS

Made in the USA
Coppell, TX
21 February 2026

72218758R00066